Gordito Haiku
BOOK ONE

BOOKS BY GORDON ANDERSON

Gordito Haiku: Book One
Gordito Haiku: Book Two
Gordito Haiku: Book Three

Gordito Haiku
BOOK ONE

360 Haiku & 60 Tanka Poems

by

Gordon Anderson

published by
ECHO SPRINGS PUBLISHING
Port Angeles, WA

GORDITO HAIKU
Book One

Copyright 2016 by Gordon Anderson
ALL RIGHTS RESERVED
Printed in the United States of America

Published by
ECHO SPRINGS PUBLISHING
Port Angeles, WA 98362
Email: echospringspub@gmail.com
www.echospringspub.com

Paperback ISBN: 978-0-9976113-0-4
Library of Congress Control Number: 2016908752
Also available as a Kindle Book

Book designed by Ruth Marcus

Set in Palatino

No part of this publication may be reproduced or transmitted to any form or by any means, electronic or mechanical, including photocopy, recording, or any information storage and retrieval system, without permission in writing from the publisher.

*This book is dedicated
to the readers of haiku.*

Contents

Preface   ix

Haiku

Chapter One	1
Chapter Two	23
Chapter Three	45
Chapter Four	67
Chapter Five	89
Chapter Six	111

Tanka

Chapter Seven	133
Chapter Eight	149

Preface

MY HAIKU AND TANKA POEMS paint pictures
with words. I set a scene, give an observation,
raise a question, and present a thought or dream.
And I write of occurrence and happening, of
man's spiritual, mental, emotional and physical
self. I deal with nature and the physical world—
life and death—and of man's survival. My focus
has been on all of these subjects.

    Each reader is unique. And to all my readers,
I think you are wise. You decide what you like.
May you experience some haiku moments.
Enjoy the poems.

x

Chapter 1
Haiku

In rainforest woodlands
under tree umbrellas
the chanterelles grow

To look and not see
a deeper and deeper whole
beyond the given scene

One needs sustenance
like protein in the morning
to get the work done

Some multitasking
cell phone—computer—T.V.
no oneness can be

The early bird awakes
to survive another night
—he sings with delight

Grandmother told her
—there is beauty everywhere
—she had to find it

At the headwaters
today—a rainbow flexes
at the waterfall

He tapped her shoulder
she turned to look at him
—he did not know her

The first morning dew
it spreads upon the plants
like a fairy's dance

Sad songs aren't all bad
sad songs can be deceiving
—some are beautiful

One thing at a time
is just like tunnel vision
—what's now on the mind?

He went to steal food
he earned his keep instead
and he got his bread

Watch who you crusade
—despot—warlord—or false god
—I saw no true face

Mockingbird's up tonight
and mimicking everything
—with a full moon bright

The desert sun beats down
I dream of water and ice
—I may pay a price

I haven't seen a soul
on this loneliest of roads
—where might I be going?

Things not heard or seen
rains fall—seas flow—and winds blow
—secrets when one sleeps

A Roman goddess
aurora borealis
—a sun of green lights

Pacific islands
something to eat and drink
—the coconut tree

I mow my yard grass
and dream of writing a poem
—maybe a haiku

To the mountain top
he climbed the long hard path
to see—his world below

The production line
he loaded flats by hand
sweat would burn his eyes

I satisfied her wants
then my lover said to me
—I love you, Romeo

In the saguaros
awake with the owl tonight
a lone coyote howls

Days of darkness
come to every single one
—in old age and life

The honeysuckle
surrounds the arbor gate
—like too many soldiers

Winds whip and churn
I sneeze and blow my nose
—pollen in the air

On the bank fishing
and conversing with a friend
—happiness again

Hard to write for me
the long and tedious poems
give me short haiku

A long winding road
—many days and many nights
—but his life worth it

On earthly deathbeds
believers and non-believers
—most everyone prays

A ruined city
all ghettoized and slummy
finds more problems plenty

You a speck of sand
we lay under open skies
—me small like an ant

A life rewarded
is for every man to have
some sense of order

Hidden and unseen
the dead man lies in the ground
—the soul left his side

At night the frogs croak
singing their songs in the dark
to mate in the marsh

A clean window shows
the mountain covered with snow
—and keener sense of cold

There are young men—to
walk my steps and take my place
—now, that I am old

The outdoor boy knows
with autumn's end—winter comes
and the walls close in

Gravity pulls on
the earth, the moon, and tides
yes—gravity pulls

Mouse in the feed bag
an opossum on the porch
the cabin door unlatched

Walking in thick snow
moving slow like a snail
it is a tough go

No heavy thoughts
lost in night to love's light
—only romance remains

Poverty mother,
lost father—the ghetto news
the rare child yet blooms

To sustain a life
getting water from a well
is a precious thing

Shades of evening come
then comes the dark and quiet
when most birds sleep

The volcano rises
above the rain and the clouds
—to tower over me

The weathered miner
only the skeleton knows
in lost fields of gold

In feasts and famines
nature speaks but few listen
—is earth too late to save?

A size difference
giant redwood sequoias
grow small tiny cones

Chapter 2
Haiku

Board games await rain
sun does not shine everyday
—come outside and play

A shelter from storms—
fire for heat and fire to eat
—all the homeless know

The unknown traverse—
very like the dark of night
needs some sage advice

Warm days—summers done
—many moons before long suns
—cold winter has begun

When the work lies done
and things stand squared away
then comes time to play

He returns again
and again to his quiet place
by the banyan tree

Tonight this year ends
a new cycle—a new life
it is New Year's Eve

The woodsman's castle
nothing more than logs of wood
—this his shelter good

A new day would come
—she lived for tomorrow
—just like her grandmother

He can hear the calls
to the right and to the left
which way does he go?

His vision blocked
from very much consternation
—will he know danger?

Safety needs thick ice
on the sled ride home tonight
—please no thin lake ice

More repetition
of needed winter chores
done—before the spring

His mind—not enough
—he had to learn to know love
with matters of his heart

The morning comes with
a chirp—a peep—a tap tap
—birds at the feeder

Stay bundled warm
more clothes—way better than none
in an outdoor freeze

Care and nurturing
of many ideas can grow
into a country

Clean water drops fell
continually from the leaf
to the lapping tongue

My dear loved friend
in time you may well forget
but for me—not yet

Careless treatments can
lead to lazy, dumb and wild
—bringing up a child

The lonely hermit
in his singular retreat
loved his singing birds

Legs had given out
but her wit kept on laughing
and dreams kept coming

He died in his sleep
but his journey did not end
—his soul traveled on

A heavy rain fell
lightning flashed—thunder roared
—he found safe harbor

The night came alive
the moon and stars shined
with his woman's love

Rain fills potholes
to form puddles in the road
—watch out where wheels go

The right direction
gave him hope and he went on
to climb more mountains

A tug on the line
—will a fat fish be hooked
and nicely netted?

What does separate
a winner from a loser
—but a winning bet

The worm a clear choice
for making compost—catching fish
—but not dinner's dish

Instantaneous
gratification is just
a type of spoiled

When the sun rises
upon everyone's house
all beacons will shine

The soldiers eat rice
—without rice in soldiers' bowls
a bad emperor dies

April brought showers
inverse—you came in the fall
and died this new spring

That warm summer eve
on the beach—just you and I
—my dream did come true

Money in the hand
customers come through the door
for products in demand

The birds take cover
and pray for better weather
when storms abound

Flowers do not grow
at the end of this last road
—adios my friend

Do not bother me
—bother me when I want to
—but that is not now

A pack of wolves
—an elk surrounded to kill
—full bellies tonight

A garden needs care
some praying—with toil and work
or weeds will take over

The high speed cheetah
and the long running gazelle
—today lived the gazelle

One favors apples
the other his cherries
—a matter of choice

Grandfather told me
when the maple sprouts its leaves
then it's time to plant

Smoked salmon bakes
and hung salmon sun dries
—two ways Indian done

Up the mountain path
he stopped to catch his breath
and looked for hours

Avalanches come
—stay out of the deep high snows
—avalanches roll

Pickers in the fields
until the crops are plucked
sunrise to sunset

To baby eaglet
it is a matter of trust
and of dependence

No need for a fire
this is not north Alaska
—it's warm Tahiti

Chapter 3
Haiku

A new butterfly
a caterpillar and a moth
cling to the same branch

Our universe lives
sun and moon stop at nothing
—and the earth spins on

High up in the firs
little hummingbirds fly
where they breed—nest—and hide

In his daily life
he gave back what was given
—did the righteous man

Where road kill abounds
there are fat eagles and crows
all hanging about

The charcoal ash white
a glass of wine—summertime
and ready for steak

In creosote plants
live the beetle, mouse, and rat
in desert valleys

The Dutchman visioned
under straw hat and worn coat
—at easel outside

On caldera floor
lives the Yellowstone River
and geysers and bears

Keeping his balance
squirrel walked his tightrope
with a nut heading home

A sudden surprise—
it can take one's breath away
with half of a chance

A lone raven eats
from a mound of rotting meat
in a frozen field

The invasive plants
on both sides of the road
—have taken over

The concert went on
his music under the floor
—the cricket chirped

That place which is plain
demands a clean—simple mind
to get to pure state

A quake shakes the earth
—rumbles and tumbles along
—in seconds it's gone

Men—women—children
—hear them sing their work chants
in labor camps—still

With help from bees
the blossoms become fruits
each year—that I eat

A matter of taste
to live in the olden days
—romantic escapes

The times have gone sour
—with each day a new beggar
out on my corner

Do you hear me now?
I stumble through forests deep
—with nature I sleep

I go the same path
to the same woods and stream
—to watch the changes

Learn sounds of the night
a yip, a howl and a hoot
—then fear will not be

I see her white flesh
the wind blows her summer dress
—I just love the wind

Bird feeder empty
the squirrel feeder broken
—what came in the night?

A new tomorrow
a new day of repetitions
—will something new come?

I go to the beach
to have a conversation
alone with myself

In a rain's downpour
a man prays at a tombstone
—somber and alone

The hummingbird goes
darting from flower to flower
from here—and to there

In the winter time
where do all the homeless sleep?
—the nights are so secret

Dreams of summer time
this winter's too cold and long
—when comes the spring thaw?

First the trees and brush
then the house burned for fire
—now left—a barren island

On foot he walked
a different path—to see
new—and welcome change

The baking of bread
—wonderful smells drift about
—but not ready yet

With pleasure or pain
alone in the wilderness
—one will not forget

Relative to rice—
corn comes from giant grass
and grows large sweet ears

I feel like a king
to bathe in a hot springs
under the moonlight

I am a weak man
I have to pray and think
and focus on strength

In Oregon forest
about a dark-eyed Junco
—she composed a song

Grandmother sings
and I listen intently
to her profound words

With my thoughts of you
I lay awake in the dark
—I can't forget you

Everyday people
opportunities for all
should be a mantra

Scraps—ash—leaves—grass—trash
do make very good compost
with help from the worm

One, two, three wavelets
over my feet at the beach
while four seagulls squawk

Not just any rose
but a pretty home grown rose
for someone special

Country time beckons
—I do not mean the music
—a walk to the spring

Emotions run wild
lovers apart reunite
—a good type of wild

A cherry blossom's bloom
it always surprises me
—nature's perfection

Those wonderful thoughts
of spry youth and fancy free
now come back to me

Tonight calm winds blow
with sand—and sea—and the moon
—here I wait for you

Chapter 4
Haiku

In the dark of night
most jungle animals sleep
—but for predators

I can't resist you
—you are the love of my life
the light of my heart

Outside my window
pitter-patter, pitter-pit
a gentle rain falls

The flute does wail
for lost and gone native sons
way out in the west

On Grand Canyon edge
he sits and waits for the sun
—for day to begin

Forever at it
—people just like ants and bees
go colonizing

Just let things go
and put away this and that
go follow a dream

On the mountain ridge
I hear voices in the wind
—I have been cleansed

A war is over
soldiers fallen and graves dug
—and a new war begins

Tree on riverbank
a leaf floats on the water
like a holy boat

My pet little flea
you, a nuisance and bother
—you never leave me

The rain forest wakes
through mist comes the rising sun
—the trees all perk up

I hear the birds tweet
chitter-chatter back and forth
—the meeting of minds

Outside catching rays
with no clouds—the sun is out
—this makes my day

The happy couples
in the nature of things
—the birds and the bees

Why is the answer
to the question: Why?—always
because of something?

The cat caught the mouse
the cat did not eat the mouse
—he played with it

So orderly—nature's
lights: the sun, the moon, and stars
how they come and go

Dandelions grow
in most every lawn and field
—a pesky salad green

I think of you—father
every time I see a train
—how you loved your work

To mineral soil
the forest fire did burn
—later came green growth

The best shrimp and grits
are down in Charleston Town
deep down in the south

To all worldly things
earthly life is limited
—but for the spiritual

It was but a shack
but it was his beloved home
—he cried to see it gone

Fair weather so still
under the moon shining bright
—a quiet peaceful night

Alone means alone
without someone anymore
all things solitary

Without a warm fire
one cannot see—only feel
—weather after dark

Tree stumps stand today
where majestic trees grew before
—now ugly barren hills

Watching for the light
only one sailor saw it
—in the dark of night

Coo-coo—coo-coo-coo
the male dove calls from his post
alone—he still sings

The ice and the snow
and the freezing cold—but yet
a livable place

If one can survive
an inner urban city
—one can survive anywhere

What lies under cover?
maybe he should take a look
—maybe open the book

Over Sedona
a mighty eagle flies
—and then it is gone

The lady comes
—the Spirit Lady comes
talking in tongues

I saw the wild duck
—the one with the yellow eyes
at the river today

Say it over and over
—there will be peace again
—say it over and over

'Closed' the sign read
—no longer in life's business
—I've been dead three years

He opens the door
and there is no one at home
—just empty again

Engage your bias
—where are you coming from?
—where are you going?

The mosquito—it
listens to Lady Silence
out over the lake

By the hands of time
I was brought into this world
and they will take me out

Wars may well result
—concentrated poverty
taking most the blame

My father calls me
—his native tongue cries and wails
—where have wild things gone

Down at the trout stream
he cast his fly to the pool
in hopes of a meal

Take a deep—deep breath
hold it in—and meditate
—now exhale—relax

Jobs and a living wage
what all the people desire
—not endless poverty

Throughout his lifetime
nothing helped him more than
—his accomplishments

One lady watered
the spring flowers on the porch
—one lady smelled them

Another page to write
and another page to read
—will study ever cease?

Chapter 5
Haiku

It is a nice day
he feels sun warmth on his skin
—he works in his garden

A calm day can change
to violent storms and rains
where Mother Nature reigns

Like so many ants
people come and people go
along their daily paths

The rabble-rousing
continued with raised fists
—the preacher preached

The pawnbroker said—
it's one thousand for this ring
—it's all bona fide

Trees stand still—no wind
everything is calm and quiet
—before the new storm

The mockingbird sings
in the eve and the morning
—the mockingbird sings

One has not a choice
—it is the luck of the draw
—one's mother and father

In our earthly way—
the sun comes out half a day
—and then comes the night

Mount Tahoma looms
high above the clouds and trees
—I in the foothills

He sat on the floor
now—inspired by silence
—he thought no more

From flower to flower
with its freedom of flight
the butterfly—floats

To grandma's fiddle
the little children played
—they danced and sang

Waves tumble and roar
to the shore they come—one by one
not ever stopping

'Open' the sign read
—forget your troubles—come in
and rest awhile

Under the clouds
the sun dances on the water
—before it goes down

A bagpipe moans
across the lake and moor
—grandfather is gone

Leaves—red, orange and gold
—autumn's in the air and trees
here in upstate Maine

Once winter has gone
I'm alive and I'm kicking
—all ready for spring

Morning comes again
sun reflects off rocky rapids
—at the river's edge

Of most importance
between man and his landscape
—is the interplay

That rascal raccoon
—he emptied the bird feeder
and stole cat's food—again

Struggle on wee one
there is a long road ahead
—your road has just begun

Down in Mexico
I loved my senorita
—now, she's gone away

Nothing but sand on
the savannah—a desert
—the foliage gone

Sometimes things don't last
a broken heart will tell you
—love is not all true

Who is the master?
God or the universe?
—but one and the same

A bright darting star
came into his life last night
—as he star gazed

Little mouse awake
he must know—where cat is at
and lookout for mouse trap

Wise mother can skin,
butcher, and cook a chicken
—also write a book

December night comes
a winter's tale with morning's light
—all things white and bright

We stay together—
she puts up with me a lot
and I her bitching

Awake with snowflakes
he appreciated morn
—and his winter land

The dogs hear his voice
he brings the sled to a stop
—dogs still want to run

In uncertainty
he always guessed with his head
—right or wrong—he guessed

Daffodils and tulips
the northwest springtime has come
—greetings with the sun

With his sack and cane
hunting shells and sea watching
—an old man beachcombs

In the misty dew
spider's web is beautiful
—just when morning comes

He worries too much
he sits and prays to the moon
—to most everything tonight

Crow testing his wings
not old enough to fly yet
—remains in its nest

What need for hard work?
sun beats down relentlessly
—he takes a siesta

To all his senses
a sexy woman in love
with him—everything

Trials and errors
and mistakes on one's road
—they all lead to growth

The sun brightly shines
—he eats his morning breakfast
outside with no rain

Robin on alert
when night crawler shows his face
robin has his feast

Stupidly staring
he looked at the flowers
—not knowing them there

She lucky with age
smiles inside her wrinkled face
now—older than most

It is a good day
for summer's heat—sweat—and toil
—and to feel the soil

The pup hears the feet
master at the door—pup barks
—he's ready to play

Mother lay in sand
as I built my sand castle
while father swam

Chapter 6
Haiku

Dreamscapes come and go
as he drifts in and out
of his pleasant sleep

Life with no self-guilt
—he left his self-righteousness
and walked away

The hornets fly free
with no enemies in sight
—not even the bees

Where are his roots?
his most comfortable place?
—the place he calls home

What are they doing?
how are they spending their time?
—lost children at night

It must be summer
ripe tomatoes on the vine
—fresh salad tonight

Not forever
it is all momentary
—these hard times in life

Clear ice that looks white
a hexagonal crystal
each snowflake unique

Dear mother has gone
but butterflies come
—winter's become spring

Aimless and confused
the wayward boy settled
to become a man

One's staying power
—ability to press on
is consistency

All seasons do end
—all flowers wither and die
—as one day will I

Laughing calls at night
the loon on the lake—the moon
—the summer begins

Too much on his plate
he cannot control his world
—too much on his mind

Her sewing thimble
holds her precious stone
—her hiding place

An empty stomach
—to be to the point and blunt
—makes all else empty

To control this earth
just foolish man's vanity
—he thinks he's the boss

In one's old age
—still thinking fine thoughts
is a true blessing

Came the town crier
walking the streets with his lamp
—he spreading the news

I am no 'Veggie'
I start out my day with ham
or bacon—and eggs

Fly poles are ready
—mayfly duns ride the waters
—the trout rise to feed

Some barbecued meat
tortillas and refried beans
—I love Mexico

Early spring garden
nothing but faithful rhubarb
—most dependable

With much noise making
a drunken sailor—tried to
tiptoe aboard

I saw Mount Shasta
once covered with deep snow
now—a snowless peak

All the snows have gone
early flowers smell so sweet
—winter becomes spring

The steelhead jumped
out of the water for the fly
—to see me on the bank

He outward stoic
—his dreams sweet and revealing
—love was in his heart

Patterns of the sun
all in God's artistry done
and colors of the moon

Forever drifting
the dreamer sat on a hill
and sang out his thoughts

Firefighter in ash
was covered top to bottom
—except for his speech

Early this morning
birdbath has a visitor
—wet bee on a leaf

Dancing waters fall
on steep descent—to splash below
where I bathe in pool

Cold winds from the north
—the eagle screams and leaves
heading south this eve

Please—lay down your guns
—peace is a simple thing
—prayed the old soldier

He listened to wind
the old man—talked to the wind
—he was a wind man

Rider was tossed
—the horse spooked and jumped
—wasp under saddle

I crave for water
I must find it—and then boil it
before I drink it

Life on earth is short
—be nice to all friends and pets
—you may meet again

The river's mantra
—downstream flowing and going
—its beat goes on

The bottled message
out sailing the sea tonight
drifted to somewhere

Photosynthesis—
I mowed grass yesterday
—today more grass grows

This October night
only he—the cat—and owl
—prowl out with the moon

When blue jays chatter
they say time for peanuts
and mischief amok

'Whatever'—is absurd
it's such a dastardly word
—a ridiculous word

Meandering path
she walks refreshed again
through green woodlands

God bless my camper—
the soothing evening breeze—
and my down pillow

The earth breathes life
as if an eternal dance
—it never sits still

Out in Nevada
beyond the fence and Fish Springs
—wild horses run free

His meetings with friends
always gave cherished moments
and times not forgot

Chapter 7
Tanka

Many rain drops fall
on a desert floor once more
water fast appears
as many raindrops combine
in a heartbeat—a flash flood

There now—dry your eyes
don't be upset little man
things will get better
everything will be okay
Rome was not built in one day

Alive is not dead
depending on one's time
—dead is not alive
depending on one's life
—all of this by God's design

I lived my life
the sun rises as usual
it is my last one
it is my last sunset—too
goodbye—I now leave this place

If kettledrums call
one may learn to play them
it just takes practice
just feel the beat and practice
Carnegie Hall is waiting

Open liquor store
the old church a halfway house
food store now—dope den
look what poverty let in
—is this not deadly sin?

Oh, banana slug
you have no wings—you crawl slowly
how did you do it?
how did you get on my roof?
—and did it take you a year?

Grandson to grandpa—
when will all the leaves fall?
when strong winds blow this autumn
when will that be?
only the good Lord knows

Across dewy grass
the slug trail winds like a snake
but no doubt lucent
—a slug path to be sure
it skips and disappears

Racing down through hills
in southern California
come dry—hot winds
from the Upper Mojave
—the Santa Ana winds blow

Today's cities
are so industrialized
—today's giant farms
automated—modified
and much subsidized

Below mountains high
above the desert plateaus
lived the Pueblo peoples
in their Mesa Verde homes
in southwest Colorado

You know what I want
give me some of that sweet stuff
give me some of that
I've got to have you tonight
give me some of that sweet stuff

He had no worries
without urbanization
in a simpler life
when he became a caveman
and drifted back into time

She may never know
—she does possess a special gift
of giving kindness
those who know her feel blessed
—they know she's better than the rest

Could be déjà vu?
I've got to be on my toes
—this closeness to you
—temptation comes to call
I'm back in the danger zone

Oh, medicine man
you and your feathered headdress
do you hear me call
to you in your jungle home
can you cure what ails me?

Jimmie had magic
his guitar laughed and cried
he was creative
he mixed rock with the blues
his music kissed the sky

In big tree valleys
in his rain forest home
—lives the black raven
among the steepled cones
—amid the mossy boughs

Those who serve and don't
—what is national unity?
—and what is just cause?
—a country togetherness
of one and all involved

The wild flowers grow
between the mountains and sea
where meadows run free
—she goes to these fields with me
we dance in flowers carefree

Gun loaded for bear
a grizzly out and about
he is on the prowl
—he is the bear that I fear
that big brown—is hanging out

Echo Springs tells me
I am once again at peace
—in tranquility
—I'm back in nature's spell
—my healing and needing place

The hard frozen snow
—Christmas morning on the go
—bringing presents home
freezing cold—twenty below
I pray for no more storms

Outlaws lie in graves
with the good—the bad—and ugly
—and a few great men
—reading tombstones—he did the math
of when they had all come and gone

Hard labor he did
his life was a rocky world
he was a man lost—
he had no computer skills
—one man in a changing world

In the summertime
Okanagan sunflowers
bloom in the east cascades
among the rolling hills
with yellow petals flashing

He learned from books
and he learned as he went
he kept on learning
—he learned from his lovers
—and from nature—his common friend

When violence comes
—when white rose turns blood red
robbers—and killers
—thieves—racists—and terrorists
all become exploding bombs

Competition and
greed wrestled—compassion
and cooperation
with three percent of the world
winning again—nothing's changed

Chapter 8
Tanka

In fog—wind—and rain
the North Head Lighthouse stands
—lights on dusk to dawn
warning ships of sand and surf
at Columbia's mouth

Dirty tramp at door
he begs for soap—not food
he wants to be clean
—with water hose and soap bar
—he scrubs himself in my yard

Oh, where might he be?
on a highway of cars?
he awakes in the dark
—or a rumbling train he hears
—maybe the ocean roaring near?

Along the river
tree leaves over rushing water
—they dance in the wind
—all a glitter with sunlight
on this summer's shining day

Beggars and peasants
the destitute and homeless
they go hand in hand
living life on a shoestring
nonmaterial to the max

Sunset Kalaloch
out beyond the driftwood beach
on the horizon
where the sky meets the sea
a fading sun disappears

He spoke his wisdom
—there is no beginning or end
just deeper contact
with the eternal beyond
and one's love for nature

In prison or not
some men and women write poems
—be poor or be rich
some people have words to say
for the good of man and country

No water and weak
lips dry and parched from thirst
the sun beats—hot desert
—a blue wavy sea in distance
is that a mirage he sees?

Enjoy the moment
nothing remains as is for long
—time frames jump quickly
all things are transitory
here today—gone tomorrow

I am thankful for
tiny animals transparent
in the deep blue sea
—all food for fish—whales—and me
—without them—I may not be

Not the cold far north
—he hungered more sunlight
and Mexico's warmth
—he learned to speak Spanish
then he traveled south for good

In ivory towers
the teachers and students become one
showing off knowledge
—the wordage made serve to them
without the nitty-gritty

At one with nature
in the middle of the night
—he crazy or not
under the moon's reflection
—he swims naked with the fish

I'm in heaven
everything's copacetic
right where I'm at
I think I'll just settle
—this place called satisfied

For perpetual help
don't pass up this free offer
—eternal life policy—
one can be saved again
all that's needed—honest prayer

Practice more practice—
guru—don't hand me that jive
—meditations take time
I have family—I have wife
—how many hours—in my life?

Morning comes with sun
he cooks breakfast by the lake
where he sits and eats
—mosquitoes swarm around his plate
—mosquitoes bite him on his face

The sun—sand—and sage
on the road to Las Vegas
to see the bright lights
down the vanishing highway
—tonight does come Sin City

He's got a new heart
he's got two new eyes and ears
and two metal knees
he's smiling ear to ear
—from all of his surgeries

Driving in thick fog
everything hides in my sight
undefined views
just silhouettes and shadows
—I can't see distinctly

Inner self—my soul
my inner self—my real self
will not let me drift
—my inner self sustains me
—it is my faith within me

Windows on the World
North Towers, 2001
people eating food
—World Trade Center all destroyed
—the Twin Towers one by one

He's the lucky one
he has fun—both—day and night
he's the lucky one
—making music—is his work
—he love's his livelihood

He cries to the trees
to the animals he bawls
—shaman's wailing calls
with his rattles and his moans
—he chants for higher wisdom

Sex—age—color—race
do not matter in any case
—when it's death to face
—under sod—all dead will lay
unless be ash—and blow away

Where the wheatgrass grows
Columbia River rolls
by apple orchards
to the orcas in the sea
—Washington State all for me

What is survival?
to stay well—live long—be safe?
what are the secrets?
no bills—no having the blues
—lots of luck—and silver spoons?

The waves much too big
—a sudden weather change comes
I must row in now
—I'm out too far on the lake
with hope—I am not too late

The farmers planted
and the life of man went on
—the warriors killed
and more mayhem came about
—what is a warrior-farmer?

Paperback and Kindle books
Available on Amazon.com

Paperback books also available
from echospringspub@gmail.com
and www.echospringspub.com

www.ingramcontent.com/pod-product-compliance
Lightning Source LLC
Chambersburg PA
CBHW051650040426
42446CB00009B/1063

9780997611304